To my dear, s...
birthday with...
admiration, l...
Have the happiest of birthdays,
and the loveliest year!

To: Dawn

From:

On your birthday I would like to propose a toast to the lender of socks, the trimmer of hair, the sharer of chocolate bars.
I wish you a day filled with smiles and surprises, and a year of adventures and excitement!
To my sister!

Age is a delusion. Do not count
the years – or even triumphs and
disasters. They cannot touch the
life within you. Those who love
you scarcely notice the marks of
time. They see only the girl still
shining through your eyes –
unharmed and beautiful.

A sister's motto:
Help first. Recriminations later.

—◇—

Who can you call at three in the
morning, stuck at the airport,
marooned by snow, covered in
spots or jealous or jilted –
abandoned and nowhere to go?
Your sister.

—◇—

Telling a sister your troubles
involves less hassle than telling
anybody else. For one thing – she
usually saw them coming.
Probably warned you.
For another, she's disentangled
you from various catastrophes
before. Many, many times.
She'll not waste time with words
– but get down to practicalities.
Which may entail a bed for the
night, a loan, a doctor, a lawyer.
Or simply some shrewd and
uncomfortable advice.

—◇—

Sisters know when to yell at you
– and when to hug.

Do you remember…?
Those are the words that are the
key to all we mean to one another.
Our little world – the world that
no one knows but you and me. A
world that's always waiting for us
to come back. Mud-flats, shining
and slithery under a summer sun.

Toboggan tumbles in the snow.
Secrets whispered bed to bed.
Near-disasters Mother never
knew about. However old we
become, however staid and
sensible – something of us still
roams that far-off land of
childhood. Together.

Some sisters are so alike as to be
near-twins – and some could be
members of two different
families.
But even then, a casual gesture,
a turning of the head, a smile,
reveals the link. We share our
lives – as we have always done.

It's good to go out with friends,
admirers, lovers – but, maybe
best of all, it's good to spend the
day with a sister.
No need to impress – she'd only
laugh. No need to hide a sniffle,
a stomach ache, a broken heart.
She takes you as you are.

Has a store of tissues and peppermints. A listening ear.

—◇—

What would I do without you? You know all my fears and weaknesses, all my secret hopes and dreams. You share my memories.

The difference between a
friend and a sister is that
with a sister the link is
indissoluble. Whatever the
stormy disagreement between
you, whatever is said in the heat
of the moment – she's always
there on the far side.

Today's the day for "Do you
remember?"
… We hold the family's history.
We talk a shorthand that no one
else can understand.
We have known each other for so
long, and so well, we need not
finish sentences.

Siblings are strangely linked –
like Siamese twins whose bond is
invisible, intangible, yet strong as
steel. We know the hows and
whys of one another. We are
involved in everything the other
does. We war at times – but need
each other, to be whole.

We've come a long way together –
and shared the hardships and the
happiness we've met along
the road:
You are the best of company.
The most honest of friends.

If you were to vanish, part of me
would vanish with you. However
much we disagree I need your life
to interlock with mine, to know
you share my secrets and my
joys. To know that you are there
– linked to my life by memories.

———◇———

Put two or three siblings together
on a sofa with a photograph
album, and listen.
"Look at your hair. I've never
seen such curls."
"Well, look at you. Panties down
to your knees. And your eye
looks funny...."
"That's where I hit it when you
pushed me off the swing.
That can't be Billy...."
"You made him wear your
flowery hat. Lord – look at you
in that swimsuit!"
"That was when you had no front
teeth and Grandma told you not
to smile."
It doesn't matter what their ages
are – childhood is yesterday.

Women grow old and wrinkled.
But not sisters. We only put on a
disguise that fools the world, but
not our siblings.
We smile at one another, sharing
the joke. For you are always the
girl I knew in childhood.
Forever young.